Dear Diana and Matthew,

The Rain on Cruise's Street

EDWARD O'DWYER

Hoping so much you'll enjoy my poems.

All best wishes,

Edward O'Dwyer

Published in 2014 by
Salmon Poetry
Cliffs of Moher, County Clare, Ireland
Website: www.salmonpoetry.com
Email: info@salmonpoetry.com

ISBN 978-1-908836-81-6

COVER IMAGE: *Cobbled Road* © Pkruger | Dreamstime.com
COVER DESIGN & TYPESETTING: *Siobhán Hutson*
Printed in Ireland by Sprint Print

*Salmon Poetry gratefully acknowledges the support of
The Arts Council / An Chomhairle Ealaoín*

Acknowledgments

Acknowledgement is due to the magazines, journals and anthologies below, as well my gratitude to their editors, for previously publishing some of the poems, or versions of them, featured in this collection:

Poetry Ireland Review, THE SHOp, Revival, The Colour of Love (ed. John W. Sexton), *Crannóg, Southword, Wordlegs, Wordlegs: 30 Under 30, Boyne Berries, The Galway Review, Outburst Magazine, The Stony Thursday Book* (#6, ed. John Liddy and Liam Liddy; #7, ed. Thomas McCarthy; and #9, ed. Mark Whelan), *Revival Trio, The Clare Champion, Census 3: The Seven Towers Anthology* (ed. Eamonn Lynskey), 'New Irish Writing' in *The Sunday Tribune, Poetic Humour, Scottish Poetry Review, The Reiver's Stone: An Ettrick Forest Press Anthology* (ed. Graham Hardie), *Agenda, The Journal, Weyfarers, The Honey Land Review, Danse Macabre, WestWard Quarterly, A Hudson View Poetry Digest, Imitation Fruit, The Blue Hour Magazine, The Blue Hour Anthology* (ed. Moriah LaChapell and Susan Sweetland Garay), *Illogical Muse, Gloom Cupboard, Forge, The Weekenders Magazine, Best Poems Encyclopaedia, The Houston Literary Review, Shot Glass Journal* and *Tinteán*.

A special thank you goes to Dominic Taylor for producing a poetry scene in Limerick, without which this book might not exist. Thank you also to Bertha McCullagh and Mairtin O'Briain for their positive influence during the book's formative years. Many thanks to Billy Ramsell and Luz Mar Gonzalez-Arias for their very helpful feedback. An immeasurable thanks goes to Eileen Sheehan, who convinced me my writing was more than a hobby.

Contents

To my parents, Marian and Gerry

Just By Chance

This is the place we have been coming to since,
this is the hour, and yet just by chance

that the stars were out that first night, and their light,
    just by chance,
glittering on the Shannon's lurching surface,

a near-full moon suspended over the centre of Thomond Bridge
just by chance of where we were stood on the quay.

And just by chance it was the most brittle silence
with which we had no words to shatter

did I think to remove my coat and place it over your shoulders,
brushed your neck with my fingers just by chance of how they shook.

Then, surely, it was just by chance of the way of the tide
that a pair of swans came floating out from the bridge's far side

towards us, and so I learned that swans mate for life
just by chance you'd read it somewhere once, but couldn't
    remember where.

As though just by chance you said that did it occur to me then
I may never have a better opportunity

to kiss you than there and then, that average Wednesday
Limerick was the most romantic place ever and just by chance.

And so gently turning you round to face me,
just by chance of the arbitrary direction of a convenient wind

your russet hair all blown back and so, just by chance,
the whole of your beautiful face staring back at me,

we kissed our first kiss in that unlikeliest of ways
sometimes things happen so perfectly and yet just by chance.

The One Worry I Have With This Book

The one worry I have with this book
is the thought of my proud parents
reading it.

Realising all these years
I've had a sex life,
and all of that time out of marriage,
often even out of love.

Yes, lust soaks these pages,
will drip out of them

and down from all the shelves
and coffee tables
on which copies rest,

splash on impact.
Like so many individual gasps
of my pleasure,
my lust will explode drop by drop
on the floors
of friends, extended family,
complete strangers

and, of course, worst of all,
the parents
who think me sinless still.
Spilling inside their laps even,

the parting of pages
a dam breaking within their fingers,
a current of lust
set in full flow;

then the sweet-stale smell of détente
filling up rooms,
clinging to the walls
of the family home

where photographs of the child-me
are still hanging –
portraits of innocence.

Your Life on the Dole

Each day a little more
you're dreading walking by
the window of that *Subway*,
finding that, in it,
isn't your most recent ex-girlfriend,
still serving greasy sandwiches.
Once a week now
you're *Googling* all the names
you can remember
from that little black book you never kept,
making sure your sudden leave
hasn't been the telling factor
in any rapid rises
to fame and fortune.
But you're so sure someday,
and sooner rather than later,
will be the fruition of these fears.
That someday you will not be gasping
with relief at the words
'no results found' –
no more the reprieve in knowing
they're all still relative nobodies;
just as you left them.

Playing Guitar

Ever since the day I was just someone
in a room full of people
where a guy was playing guitar,
and where two beautiful girls
whispered, giggled and then agreed
guys who play guitar are so sexy,
I have been thinking of it;
wanting to play guitar.

I can write a poem, yes,
but it's not the same as playing guitar.
As being that guy, strumming and crooning
in a room full of people,
pretending not to overhear
when a beautiful girl
whispers to another,
who then giggles, agreeing
guys who play guitar are so sexy.

If I could play guitar,
and if I found myself playing sometime
in a room full of people
where, let's say, two beautiful girls
have just agreed it's so sexy,
then I could announce the next song
– Eric Clapton's *Layla*, for instance –
saying something like,
here's a song for all you beautiful girls,

which, after all, is more or less
word for word what I've heard said
in rooms full of people
by guys playing guitar,
and where beautiful girls

have been whispering
and giggling and agreeing
that guys who play guitar are so sexy.

But that's all if I could play guitar
and not just, instead, write this poem;
is if I was in a room full of people
and not a room by myself.
That is if I could hear the whispering,
the giggling, and the agreement
of two beautiful girls
and not, instead, this complete silence
tending to be the difference
between a guy writing a poem
and a guy playing guitar.

Fingerprint

*"Fingerprint examiners routinely testify
that they have 100 percent confidence
in their results…"*

FILMMAKER DAVID SIEGEL

As morning honeys through the blinds
to find out what has happened
and you're gone to the kitchen for coffee,
my mind is setting
bright yellow tape around the bed
– *Investigation Scene! Do Not Cross!* –

is careful doing so
not to upset an atom within,
as if prepping the area
for meticulous eyes;
the teams of hotshot detectives
and forensic specialists.

I note all the evidence piece by piece –
the shape of your head
in the flattened pillow,
the contours of your shoulders
pressed in the ragged duvet;

there, too, the impressions of bum,
heels and the faint lines of legs,
arms and back,
the deep dents of my knees and hands;
set in the fabric like putty moulds:
an imprint of the love we've made.

We'd be caught in no time,
I'm thinking to myself
just as you're entering,
two mugs in your hands,
one of them held out to me.

"How could we ever hope
to get away with it,"
I say to you, accepting the mug
and looking still at the bed;
like a fingerprint,
conclusively, undeniably ours.

Mostly For You

Love, will you come and sit
with me here a while?
It's time
I told you of my indiscretions:

I must tell you
of the other woman. Her name is Emily.
Emily Dickinson.
Maybe you've heard of her?

Love, I really do wish
I'd told you sooner of my infidelity;
of all the times, crazed with want,
I've sought out

the embrace of her *Collected Poems*.
I confess to you
the hunger of my fingers
for the worn pages,

and so often falling into such sleep,
face pressed upon them,
after the late hours we'd spent.
Oh but love,

you cannot feel jealousy,
not for Emily,
and should cast no fleeting glances
in scorn or contempt

toward her place there on the shelf.
You must swallow down
no inward sighs of loss in her name as,
my love, there is no loss,

and even now you must know
this has been a love poem
mostly for you,
only somewhat for her.

On Oscar Wilde's Visit
To Constance Mary Wilde's
Grave, Genoa, 1899

Now I see it so clearly, his huge body
slung in such sad reflection by the graveside,
the epigram of his colourless face
set 'tween long, brown locks
without the art of Beardsley's[1] brush,
etched there like the words
on the stone, beneath the marble cross
and dark ivy leaves;
not a prayer of love to her departed soul,
but rather the *Revelations*
that ends *The Book of Life:*[2]
that "nothing could have been otherwise
and life is a very terrible thing."[3]
You who knew more than any
the utter uselessness of all regrets,
yet these words, the greatest of regrets,
and certainly the most useless.

[1] Aubrey Beardsley, commissioned in 1894 to illustrate the English
translation of Wilde's 'Salome'.

[2] Adapted from dialogue between Mrs. Allonby and Lord Illingworth
in Wilde's 1892 comedy *A Woman of no Importance*.

[3] Wilde in a letter to Robert Ross, describing his visit to the grave. In:
D. Pritchard, *Oscar Wilde*, Geddes & Grosset, p.170.

Keeping

She has thought of it, of leaving the house,
starting out afresh some place far from there;
a place that never felt those footsteps;
where nothing knew that touch of hand;
where the air doesn't remember his breath.

But she thought of what she'd be leaving
if she did it, just upped and went; thought of
all the clothes, still folded in drawer-chests
and hanging up in wardrobes, from them
the unmistakeable scent since gone;

it all left undisturbed, untouched from
that day burned forever in her memory;
the time, the taste of strong tea on her tongue;
the knock, the face of the young officer
on her doorstep, cap clenched in his hands,

voice shaking in the morning chill.
Mostly, though, she thought of the shelves
on the bookcases; all the books he'd read
in his lifetime; all those pages through which
his fingers had passed, rested gently on,

smudged with their natural oils;
pages where, perhaps, flakes of skin are left
behind, preserved as a leaf or a flower
may be preserved; a piece of him; something
to stay for; worth keeping, she'd think.

Pints With God

for Dan Mooney

Meeting with God for a pint,
he should have been here
twenty minutes ago.
Fashionably late as always.

Over the years I've come to know
God can be a little vain some ways,
arrogant even – a bit
the worship-me-and-no-other type.

He's cancelled on me
the last two times we made plans,
always the same excuse –
things are hectic lately at the office.

When he gets here I'll be aloof
with him, but then God always knows
just what to say, will beg
forgive me as I would forgive you

and, with a grin, propose a toast
to forgiveness,
about to perform his favourite miracle,
turning two pints into many.

The Love They Used To Make

They both remember it very well,
the love they used to make;
the noises
they filled the bedroom with
when (once upon a time)
they would undress each other
in candlelight;
when want and desire
were burning oils,
sandalwood,
jasmine or ylang-ylang
in their nostrils.
They both remember
fingers' hunger,
when skin was silk to touch,
when flesh on flesh
was magnetic need.
And both remember
their shadows on the walls,
the perfect black of their shapes
melding to one,
moving in the rhythms
of that love,
but all once upon a time now,
no more. Yes,
they both remember it very well;
only look at each other
like they've forgotten.

'The Red Window' Poems

for Kerry Hardie

Illness kept her there

where I imagine
a bed
of sheets pulled up to chin

the room filled
by the uncertain-of-itself light
of winter afternoons

the window opened

letting in the air
and the sound

of a wind
picking itself up slowly
pained

lifting a poem
into the red frame

Library Girl

For almost a year
until I knew her name
she was the 'Library Girl' to me.

Talking with friends,
and on one boozy night a taxi driver,
I had nothing else to call a girl
I first saw
breezing through the doors
into that paper and ink universe;

who for that almost-year
had me imagining my life
as some lucky book;

had me swearing with each reverie
how easily
I'd pass a lifetime
collecting dust on a shelf,

fabric and threads
being gnawed at by mites
and a yellow fever
slowly gripping me all over,

for the chance to, just once,
pass completely,
page for page, through
those studious fingers.

As He Did

It showed up after his passing,
arrived with as much unexpectedness

and mornings now sits in the place where he sat
across from her at the breakfast table,

but has never poured coffee
or opened the newspaper, as he would.

All day, as he was, it is hardly from her side,
even before dark follows her out

to fetch coal, but does not, as he did,
carry the tin bucket inside.

And each night it comes into the bed with her,
lays beside her as he lay,

yet gives no kiss to her cheek,
turns up then in her dreams, as he did.

The Dark and the Wind

I just can't remember what youth taught me.
There was an age it abandoned me in the night;
when it left me for the dark and the wind
and so, those lessons were forever gone.

There was an age it abandoned me in the night;
the things it taught me all took off as I slept
and so, those lessons were forever gone.
Just maybe it was a windy midwinter night

the things it taught me all took off as I slept.
And no, youth left no farewell note on my pillow.
Just maybe it was a windy midwinter night
took like a thief all it had taught me,

and no, youth left no farewell note on my pillow:
it was gone, and just age there in its place –
took like a thief all it had taught me,
the night left only years to fill the gaping space.

It was gone, and just age there in its place
and, since, they're all midwinter nights now.
The night left only years to fill the gaping space:
the years came and others just kept following.

And since they're all midwinter nights now
I just can't remember what youth taught me.
The years came and others just kept following
when it left me for the dark and the wind.

The Lost Poems

Of course there are
the poems that got away,

and every once in a while
he does wonder about them;

of all the 4a.m. moments
he didn't roll from the warm bed

out into the hypothermic dark
to fumble his way

to the lamp and writing desk
in the corner of the room;

times when pen and paper
were nowhere to be found

and he trusted that fickle little voice
whispering again and again

I'll remember, I'll remember;
when the napkins-full

of magnificent phrases and images
were lost to the wash,

turned to countless fluff bits
inside a jeans-pocket;

and slipped through his fingers
like might-have-been lovers,

they are all long gone now
to some place else;

all moved on since
and probably happy-ever-after;

inevitably, he's sure,
with other poets now.

Noise

Each day he'd sit
by the piano
composing beautiful music,
the waste paper basket
beside him full with
his life's most recent work.

Some say that
when asked once who inspires him,
he answered "no one",
called Brahms,
Miles Davis
and Jan Johansson
all failures,

pausing a few seconds
before adding
that "the only task
of the musician is to create
a sound even sweeter than
the silence he breaks.
Anything less, he knows,
is mere noise."

For the past twenty years now
he's been meaning
to take an afternoon off,
call by the neighbours'
to apologise.

We'll always have Paris

We could say to ease the moment,
we'll always have Paris.
And whatever at the time that meant
let's remember here that we had such bliss.

Yes I know that now it's all so sad,
but we should find some compensatory way to look at this;
my darling, aren't you glad
we'll always have Paris,

always, for one thing, that really glorious kiss –
was it Arc de Triomphe or La Tour Eiffel?
We'll always have Paris
though the rest's gone a bit to hell,

but honey, listen – I'll explain how it's all going to be okay:
we'll always have Paris;
always have champagne on the Champs Elysees,
in spite of all the other things we're sure to miss;

always have Notre Dame,
even after this big and awful crisis;
always have the love we made because the Louvre was pretty lame.
We'll always have Paris,

complaining about how steep the Moulin Rouge is
walking back to the hotel under stars and moonlight;
we'll always have Paris,
memories to put any woes or regrets to right,

so stop, don't say it – that we were never even there – say
we'll always have Paris.
My darling, with you gone I'll be saying every day
we'll always have Paris.

Pages Missing

for Teri Murray

After the years and years
she held tightly to each of all the days
when love kissed
pain away,

but now wonders
where have all the others gone;
what became of them.

All the empty space in there;
those gaps and holes
and all this leaping to be done
to move through it,

it's as if
she's turning the pages
in the sort of book she might have written
but finding so many are missing,
torn out,

the numbers skipping and skipping,
sentences overleaf
never picking up where they left off;

as though there were reams of days
she'd balled up,

tossed away
like bad poems.

Things That Needed Saying

That's the thing with those nights,
and then that night
we both went and said those things;
the countless, innumerable things
collected up
over all those nights;
the innumerable, infinite things
we shouldn't have said
and have been
all those nights since
wishing we hadn't;
the countless things
we really didn't mean;
all those things
that needed saying
that night
just the same.

The Witch

"The number of witches had everywhere become enormous."
JOHN JEWEL

To you, strange and spurned woman
in that gloomy, crumbling old house
at the street's end,

the one with the high
and rusting wrought-iron gates,
weed-infested garden,
and all those cats
sitting in the dirty windows,

goes this, my apology,
necessary still
though all of twenty-something years late.

For listening to the story,
and for believing it.

For filling nightmares with you,
images of a slime-green face
glowing through the steam
of a big black cauldron.

For shivering at the sight
of your grey eye
peering out of a slit between the curtains.

For fearing the curse you'd put on me,
and the only real curse
the one my fear put on you.

And for spreading the story,
passing it down years after,
when I knew
it had all been just a hoax.

In the end you died, alone,
from your old age,
but for years while you lived

I was part of an awful mob,
was pinning you to a stake,
spitting flaming words on you,
watching you burn.

They Have Mistaken Me

My wife has been kidnapped.
They have mistaken me for the kind
who answers vast ransoms
by running to the bank to make withdrawals,
calling up creditors, friends, parents,
scaring up every last euro I can.
They have mistaken me for the kind
who responds to mail threats
made of cut-out-letters from magazines.
Time passing
and nothing changing hands,
they started sending me pieces of her,
sent a pinky finger first and then a big toe.
Another postage threat
that a nipple would be next
was no bluff;
it came in the velveteen case
of a ring from a fancy jeweller's,
(no doubt bought with the life
of some top banker's beautiful wife).
All these pieces being cut away,
but still the asking price has not budged.
They have mistaken me for the kind
who can be intimidated into giving in.
An ear has arrived this morning,
still wearing the pearl
she had on leaving for the shops that day.
Next might be one of her green eyes.
Or maybe it will be an arm, or even a leg,
all wrapped up carefully
in cellophane and cardboard
like a twisted birthday present.
Or who knows,
maybe next they will send the head.
Anything surely is possible when
they have mistaken me for the kind
who wouldn't have given vast sums
to have her cut up into pieces.

Summer Thought

In this kind of heat
the only gales and torrents
that blow and teem
in the sweating streets

are of beautiful girls –
onslaughts
of skin and bronze
and contour.

I find myself asking,
where were they
all those long winter months
we needed them so desperately?

Wondering,
had no-one told them
the sun, too, comes out
just to watch them go by.

The Leaves

(i) The Despair of Leaves

The mischief-making grey hands of winter
have felt up just about everything now
as there go some leaves
– perhaps even the last –
to their final dance,
but the wind no more
that silk-handed fox-trotter
of summer months,
when its every touch
had a lover's
unequivocal warmth.

(ii) *The Miracle of Leaves*

Without better explanation back then,
I decided

the wind collected them,
gathered up every last one

and, as no one was looking,
pegged them all

back on the bare arms of their trees,
its swirling moan

the whispered incantation
restoring their green blood,

mending the impossible chiropractics
of spines

without rest through days and nights
to the miracle moment

they're all back as they were,
good as new;

like they'd never
fallen to their deaths.

At a Loss For Words

(i) *Someone Else's Words*

*"Love these days usually comes
dressed in inverted commas."*

SUE HUBBARD

Let's just not bother about the words
it occurs to me to use,
let's this time
leave 'beguiling'
and 'utterly luminous' unsaid,
every facile phrase
said so often before,
and this time, this once,
spare the way
you're looking tonight
the shortcomings
of my very best words;
do this in hope and belief
the words I would use
must exist,
are, I'd expect,
hiding bashfully away
within a poem
I may or may not have ever read,
someone else's words,
as I mutely wait,
imploring the silent
and empty air between us
to produce them
out of nothing;
to slip out of
their inverted commas
and nakedly
onto the tip of my tongue.

(ii)　　*Note Following a Blank Page*

It's because even the best words
have been used so flippantly
and for things
so much less beautiful,

the poem I've dedicated to her face
– which at the time
I considered
but eventually decided not
to call 'Ode to Her Face' –
is a page left bare.

Nothing there at all
but its already perfect
and unblemished whiteness,
a space each re-reading of

leaves me recalling
my closed and frustrated
thesaurus,
nothing to add
as I sat composing blank lines.

The Song of the Tree

The forest has many trees, but I choose
this one, though it's no taller than others
and though all its leaves it'll surely lose.
Still, for now, they'll crackle when a wind stirs,

if any breeze will ever choose my tree.
I wait here for its soft green voice, to know
the threnody of its leaves – sing for me,
I whisper, words hungry for wind to blow.

Suddenly then it lets out a hushed sound,
a gentle gust choosing it now. My tree
tosses one leaf then toward my piece of ground.
There beside it I crouch down to one knee,

take it in my hands, hold it carefully –
a note from the song my tree sings for me.

Mary Ann Vecchio's Face

*(inspired by the Pulitzer Prize
winning photograph by John Filo)*

Lead splits the air in instants
but that thirteen-second volley,
sixty-seven M-1 Rifle shots,
must have seemed an endless time
there in the midst of the protest,
and yet somehow, within it,
four lives were lived all too quickly
and lost all too suddenly.
But Jeffrey Miller, William Schroeder,
Allison Krause and Sandra Scheuer
did not die without revealing a truth
so deep only bullets could expose it.
I didn't need to be in Ohio
on that May 4th to learn
that the pain and grief in such horror
has its way of freezing; still as time
in a photograph; as the distortion
in Mary Ann Vecchio's face.

Deciduous

Tell me, how does it feel?
But before you answer,
think about that tree;
remember, in the field
behind your house;
where we used to kiss,
when our feelings
were first blossoming;
where we took
a blunt knife, carved
a crude heart together
in the young bark;
where we inscribed
each other's names
on the clean insides.
If you can see all of this
then maybe you can hear
the sound of leaves
rustling together
in a tender breeze,
sharing a rhythm,
skin over skin
and sinew for sinew.
Keep going. Follow
this thought, the vision,
the sound; follow
until, ever so suddenly,
I'm there with you,
waiting in chill silence
and shed leaves,
and I'll ask you again,
how does it feel?
Does it feel like winter?
Does it feel as though love
has been stripped down
around your heart?
I know. I feel it too.

The Muse in Moskva

It was in Moskva
and an impregnable winter,
blue-eyed and wrapped in all her furs,
I found her, or she found me,
and we downed too many vodkas
toasting the 'good old days'.

She took me out walking in the Kremlin,
brought me to the Church of Laying Our Lady's Holy Robe
and told me of its legend of the Virgin,
to the Archangel Michael's Cathedral,
telling the hidden histories
of interred tsars,

and shoving through
the belligerent blitz of a dusk snow,
we stood finally in whitest Red Square,
she whispering poems
like sweet nothings in my ear,
slipping, then, her arm
through the loop of mine,
my pen throbbing
for paper.

The Joy Life Can Be

My beautiful girlfriend says
the happiness we've found
in finding each other
is not something to be celebrated only
beneath sheets and duvets,
or behind the drawn curtains
or the closed door;
when we're sure there's no one looking.

No, no, she says it must be shared,
the sight and even sound and scent of it
released at every opportunity
into this sad and lonely world,
ever so desperately in need
of belief
in our kind of pure
and absolute happiness.

She says it's nothing short of our duty
to walk through these streets
holding hands, smiling widely
and gazing warmly
into one another's eyes,
never looking where we're going,
sure that all these shoppers
out buying their contentments
will step aside
to watch as we breeze by.

She says a passionate clinch
and kiss with plenty of tongue
smack-dab in the middle
of a crowded, public place
can only do a world of good
to share what we have,
not a sliver of daylight
between our ripe, young bodies

and, as an example of this,
often refers back
to the time outside the bus station,
unaware as the rain began coming down,
we held each other so closely
and so intensely
for what must have been a full thirty minutes,
that staring, hopeless wino
suddenly believing in it, realising
the joy life can be.

The Future

When the summer arrives (late as ever),
by then you've forgotten
why you awaited it
so expectantly.
As it comes flouncing into the horizon
suddenly you can remember
nothing of why you thought the winter
such a disagreeable bastard,
then find yourself pleading
with daylight to recede,
sun to vanish,
take with it the garish glow
it's given everything,
including your own skin.
Suddenly now you're ready to admit
that you've fantasised in autumn
of putting all the leaves back
on the stick–limb trees,
one by one paint them all green
if that's what it takes;
how there were springs
you dreamt of
running through meadows
stamping each and every blossom
back into the dirt it rose up from.
You're ready at last now
to stare the future in the face,
see the lie in its winning smile
and bedroom eyes:
the absolute certainty
that, the moment it finally turns up,
it will have already broken
every promise it ever made.

Visit from a Poem in a Dream

She came first in a dream,
this woman
most beautiful of beautiful women.
But there she said:
"I am not a woman but a poem."
And so I asked her then:
"Why do you come to me
in a woman's form?
Why have you not come here in words,
as metaphor and as rhythm,
as structure and as imagery?"
Just then her eyes changed,
turning equally
to pity, to cruelty and to sorrow
as she answered:
"Because I am a poem
never meant to be written.
From this day forward
you will be seeing quite a lot more of me
and yet never as words.
In your life and your dreams
I will turn up again and again.
At dinner you'll see me
in the arc of your lover's shoulder,
sipping seductively at a glass of red wine.
In the streets
you will catch whiffs from the breeze
of my unmistakable perfume.
But I am yours only,
no other will ever notice
as at will I slip in and out of view
in a crowd's midst.
I will be the poem you'll always feel
you can write

but then never will;
the one to make you curse
all the poems you do.
Even the most beautiful
will only be good as the prettiest
of these ordinary women
from this night
you'll spare none of your desire for,
and in a lifetime then
you'll know I have been your poem
for whom words were not enough;
to whom
words were all you ever
had to offer.

The Secrets in the Sea

The moon fondling the blowing sea,
its hands of light groping gently,
my love points out where water gleams;
the secrets where such lambent beams
will pry but really should not be.

None loves a secret much as she,
and she points out there, guiding me,
at thin bright fingers poking seams –
the moon fondling the blowing sea.

Watching its careful hands, I agree
secrets must be out there, at sea,
where moon runs its nails 'long the seams
and stitches, and the threads all gleam.
We stand, watch on, my love and me,
the moon fondling the blowing sea.

Things Are Always Changing

Things are always changing, this is something you'll see.
At least that much – even if nothing else – is clear,
but take no notice what and how, just let them be.

Sure, you'll never persuade time to let you live freely,
and then circumstance always has its own ideas, dear.
Things have changed, this is something you'll see

soon enough. That's why we have the word suddenly.
Can you feel them yet? Some are definitely here.
Take no notice what and how though, just let them be.

The joining of ourselves to their momentum is what's key
now; only fools use up their fight against them, dear.
Things will change again. This is something you'll see.

Have you noticed how things always find a way to be?
That change is never far; that its hand always is near?
Give no notice what and how, instead let them be,

all of these things, different futures, uncertainty.
Give your hand as they take it. Be led without fear.
Things are always changing, this is something you'll see,
but take no notice what and how: just let them be.

Climax

He's made a point
of going about sex
with her

always now
as he would
go about writing a poem:

frolicking fingers,
lick of tongue
to drive of hips,

considered
and careful
as words

seeking
a lingering gasp of pleasure
at their end.

December

He steps out into frost,
into stifling cold,
sees the land is a pallid, sad face
looking listlessly back at him;

and realises
nothing is unusual
in the trudge
through charcoal slush;

in the near slip
on an ice-patch,
in the dry crack of bone
each foot-step;

least of all the cheer
of garden Christmas lights
mocking
another year in the attic.

The Rain on Cruise's Street

Right now
I'm envying the rain on Cruise's Street.

And it occurs to me
I'm probably the only one,

but I am in no hurry
as shoppers
rush between Claire's and Boots
as it heavies and thickens

and the clouds overhead
groan machinelike.

And yet my envy
I could pinpoint down
to a single
and isolated drop.

This one,
I could scapegoat for the rest

as they come down,
lashing the faded red-brick
in torrents,
turning it a muddy brown.

That full and luscious drop.
That one right there,
see it?

The one trickling
down her neck
like a lover's liquid tongue.

A Corpse in Snow

Her parents gave her the name Summer,
remembering at the hospital

the kind nurse with round glasses and big smile
who called her Sunshine.

In an always-full maternity hospital,
maybe she called all the babies this.

Now just seventeen years old,
here she lies, just a corpse in snow,

limp-stiff,
naked flesh turned powder-blue

and eyes dilated, stricken,
a meaningless struggle stark

in the pink rawness of her slender wrists
and in the pale contusion

on her jaw; in the gaping wound
below her chin –

the clean slice
of a Winter's frozen blade.

For them, whoever they were

For them, whoever they were,
let us join together here and now,
raise this glass,
make this toast.

For all those
no more recognisable
as a fart on a faraway wind;

they that never warranted a pedestal,
or even sweeping
under history's rugs.

For the dedication of their whole lives
to the staunch pursuit
of saying nothing,
doing even less,

make this toast,
raise this glass –
let us join together here and now
for them, whoever they were,

all their names, for posterity,
not collected here.

Learning to Walk

There must be a course they all do,
taken in secret.
I'm sure of it.
A universal rite of passage
at, say, that ripe age of sixteen;
a diploma equivalent
for which they disappear
into the high mountains
or deep woods
for the intensive training,
learn to walk
with books
balanced on their heads,
then fine antique vases;
to tread upon the air
a centimetre above the ground
so as never to stumble
or stub a toe
in a crack in the pavement.
I've been watching them
in the streets,
how they go by, accentuating
their exquisite shapes,
their contours
and such perfect rhythmic strides,
and each beneath
their own personal spotlight
of sunshine.
I've been watching them
as they walk
and decided this:
there must be a course
that they take.
There just must be.
I mean, are we to believe
they were just born
with their ability
to walk all over us?

Rock Chick

She listens to punk rock,
blasts it in the bedroom
of her squalid upstairs flat.

When on top
she is facing the big *Sex Pistols* poster
hung above the headboard
of her rocking bed,

ignores neighbours'
banging on the walls,
single mothers' screaming
for quiet,

he with his head pillowed
and pointed up,
eyes feasting on
the wild movements
of hair and arms and breasts.

None of them realise
she's really someplace else,
far from their wasted pleas,

that she's really front-row-centre now
at a show
playing just for her

where he, rock star, god,
is about to shout out,
"You there in the front
givin' it everythin' you've got!
This one's for you, baby!"

Thoughts Besetting the Deceased Lady Ahead of her own Funeral

She thinks
of going to her own funeral
and thinks, if ever she must look upon her dead self,
she must not do so mourning;
must not regret those last impressions
which, of course, must last.

She thinks
what shall I wear?
and what shall I do with my hair?
She feels barraged with details,
with loose ends and endless possibilities;
things to consider,
to decide on and see to.

She thinks
wouldn't it be awful to leave it all to chance?
and she hates to think
that, lying stiff in the casket,
she could somehow be there more than in body.

She thinks
what if I must take part in this grief?
and *what if I can hear all the whisperings*
from the pews?;
her family, her friends and neighbours,
business associates
and all manner of acquaintances –

she thinks
what if they don't all remark
'how beautiful she looks'?
or *'could anyone but she*
have made such a radiant corpse'?

Competing

The summer is the most ambitious
I've ever seen it,
not the absentee landlord
of other years;

in the drenched air
I can feel in my skin
its greedy hunger
for degrees Celsius

as, hand in hand,
she and I stroll
through O'Connell Street,

its yellow, jealous eye
bulging above us,
never blinking;

locked on her every sizzling move.

Autumn

Summer and winter
eye one another up
with violent intent.

Autumn is a school playground,
a frontier battlefield.

A menacing tension
hangs in the air
as leaves on trees dwindle,
remaining birds
singing only half-hearted songs
amidst the grey-blue grapple
of day-time sky.

We know too well how it turns
in an instant's instant,
just a few
congested grumbles
in the clouds
to rain flogging on roofs,
wind rattling windows,
to mist, to frost, to ice.

It is about to turn again –
any moment now,
and then the days won't let up,

revelling in the cracking of bones,
delighting in the purple-grey of skin,
singing in every ear
its numbing winter song.

And time is just for waiting then;
for awaiting;
perhaps the sight of a wasp
or butterfly indoors;
any news-bearer
of summer's survival;
its return
to contest the spring.

Paradise

You might have been Eve today
as you stood there, cream-skinned naked,
something of Eden about you
in those fields
between Shannon Banks and Parteen.

Yes, you could have been the world's mother
this sunniest of afternoons;
nature's chosen queen
as you stuffed the braids of your hair
with purple wildflowers

under sapphire-blue sky
and amidst sweet bird-song,
the bounce of sponge-grass underfoot,
the unripelling river
that went by as though at your bidding,

re-making happiness, as you were;
as an unbroken circle
we couldn't fall out of.
Yes, you really might have been Eve today,
being yourself, no more, and somehow re-making Paradise

intact again as an unbitten apple.

First Rejection

The envelope came today,
my first rejection
of poems submitted
to an esteemed literary journal;
and looking over the sparse few words
the busy editor
took the time to write
(almost illegibly)
I can't help thinking suddenly
back to that very first girl
who didn't want to go to the pictures;
who'd made other plans
she couldn't get out of;
who was booked up all week
despite my own
more than gymnastic flexibility;
she who taught me
the crush in the subtler signs
of complete and utter disinterest –
signs in words such as
"thoughtful and intriguing
but in need of a little more craft."
Nor can I help remembering now
those advices
of so many well-meaning friends;
their words of consolation.
"She isn't worth your time, mate."
"She's a bit of a cow anyway."
None of which helped then.
And they help nothing still –
another letter or an email,
a change of mind,
a reconsideration,
note of a preferred poem
having being withdrawn even,
still I'd leap at the chance
to get my piece
between its illustrious pages.

Lir's Children

*(Inspired by the monument in The Garden of Remembrance,
Parnell Square, Dublin)*

The agony and torment
is there on the faces,
the desperation in the bodies,
youth learning
the curse age alone
should teach –

that life is a sentence
of one kind or another.

And what could ever curse you
more than that?
I lift my eyes to the swans
taking flight from backs,
to the expanse of blue
behind spread wings.

I remember back to the story
read as just a child –
a tale of lakes, of prisons,
of one three hundred years of captivity
to another –

but yet watching now,
the only sentence surely
is freedom,
for no wings have ever been chains.

Kiss

The air has a taste of imminence on it,
of something almost happening,

a change ready to strike the universe,
unleash unknown forces

tilting worlds onto new angles.
The look of anticipation

on your face
says you sense it too.

It is happening.
I'm sure it's happening now,

beginning. It will be
unmistakable soon enough.

In a moment we will know what it is,
what has happened,

what has changed,
what there's no coming back from.

Girl Picks a Flower in the Park

This moment
a girl picks a flower in the park
as the sky blackens.

Her oversize yellow raincoat
insists I watch
as she turns

and shelters the single hyacinth
from rising wind,
hungry at her back,

whistling with zealousness,
scent of beautiful delicacies
in its snuffling nostrils,

but I see, for now at least,
its petals, her smile,
remain intact.

Pyre

She thinks of gathering it all up,
the finished and the failed,
all abandoned embryos,
the scribbled notes,
the first drafts and second drafts,
each of the ones floating in poem limbo,

thinks of making them a pyre,
dousing it with spirits,
striking a match in the black of night,
setting it ablaze in a blinding flash;
of starting again from scratch
in the light of its flames.

Space

Once more I've realised
the terrible lover I've been
of late;
admit to times

on cold or stormy nights
I turned away
from her soft whisper
at my ear.

And I can remember
the pinnacle of my anger,
the venom
with which at times I swore

never again
I'd have anything
to do with her.
But then my love,

the true love that she is,
knows my moods
even better than I;
knows when to let me be

to work these things out;
let me to shake
little tantrums without her,
by myself;

that soon enough
I realise my indiscretion,
will be back,
down on both knees

wanting,
craving her forgiveness,
pen and paper
in outstretched hands.

A Leaf Falls

And this is death for you,
this descent,

thoughts now only for
that waiting rigour-mortised ground.

Still, moving like a last dance,
I suppose you'd say
why not?

Tangoing,
led by unseen hands;
giving yourself to the nuances
of each moment,
making it a good one,

you never danced
as freely as this.

You who only ever knew
the summer breeze in life,
falling as if to say

why should my thoughts
be for the cold, hard, waiting ground?

Poem for a Beautiful Derriere

He remembers the days they could admire
for fully two hours
the graces of a single backside,

blustering on and on
of all the things
they'd have done with it –

so it was for virgins of seventeen,
hormones oozing
from every pimpled pore.

But he would never have imagined back then
all that gawping, the carrying on,
getting old, tedious,

could never have seen it coming and yet,
sure enough, here he is now
looking for new ways

to fill the idle hours,
for the present getting his kicks
composing poems

with dedications to a former self
and all the beautiful derrieres
he knew,

those voluptuous contours
always still out of reach,
this time from the best words he can muster.

The Great Poet's Only Complaint

So commendably he came to terms
with the awful pea-green carpets
and even worse matching sepia curtains
of an upstairs flat,

its single, mildewed window
overlooking a side of town
the sun had a falling out with years ago
(and has had nothing to do with since),

so graciously having accepted
those cold water mornings,
night's snap of mousetraps
and the weak brew of reused teabags,

this great poet's only complaint
is the trail of missed opportunities
going on for miles and miles
his life has denied him;

that long list of wonderful things
he could have been,
would have been only for
choosing not to be;

all those things
which from the pedestal of his ego
he might refer to as
the necessary sacrifices for his art;

those things without which
each poem remains
only another classic tear-jerker
without a beginning.

On The Upside

Our Lady Limerick's high-street shops
and the pubs once packed out
even on flogging Monday nights
are closing down,
the trademark Irish smirk
has suddenly slipped
with affluence getting laid off.

Penny's is the new Brown Thomas,
Dominic Street the new Cruise's Street.

And so what to do now?

Do you turn back to God
now the elastic has snapped back,
take Him up on His offer of forgiveness?
Do you re-hang your sacred heart
in the kitchen

between unemployed graduates,
go banging on the church doors
now the holes
are ever-gradually reappearing
in the kids' shoes,

now that today's bread
is always yesterday's
despite what Mr. Brennan is saying?

Should you go looking
everywhere you can
for consolation, for reprieves
and olive branches?

Is there any worth pointing out
that, on the upside,
it's raining much less
than it used?
The sunny spells in December
and March were an unexpected treat.

Meteorologists are the new economists,

it seems, as the TV3 weatherman
smiles and winks, flirts and dances
with mesmerised cameras

as if to suggest
an *Angela's Ashes*
minus all the shit weather
would not be such a downer of a read.

Book

It's the darkness
does it,

quietly
turns a page
as you're sleeping,

and then its leaving
that wakes you,

in its place
the morning

swelling with new words.

Silence

First thing next morning,
(too late), they've realised it,

all the simple talk is gone,
the unremarkable stuff
of silence-thwarted moments
and years;

taken off during the night
as they were sleeping soundly;

packed up
all its words and sentences,
its familiar prompts
and responses,
vanished into the thin air;

not so much as a farewell note
left on the kitchen table,
no clue
to where it was headed;

slipped out
without raising the bark of the dog,

leaving them to each other.

Snow

December 21st 2009

All the perfect white powders
pillowed
on cars and hedges,
spread like new duvets
over suburban gardens
all just thrown snowballs now;

and the day's excited cries
and laughter
leaving no trails behind them
as they wandered off,
vanished out
into the wilderness of silence;

and the eager morning passed,
now just jaded dusk,
no tantalising snowflakes
remaining to be kissed
from a lover's pink nose.

Poem for Someone of no Particular Importance

Though never awarded the Nobel Prize
and never shook a president's hand;

though no calendar or street
survives your name

that made the local papers
for nothing more than death,

still it shouldn't be thought
a life of nothing noteworthy at all

doesn't deserve a poem in dedication
and remembrance;

at the least, something of a beginning
that skips abruptly to an end.

This Old Pain

This old pain, it really ain't so painful these days,
though back then I'd have sworn it'd tear me apart.
But then I guess that's just another of life's funny ways

and, just maybe, time is a healer of all wounds as the proverb says,
for these are times I feel I could make a brand new start.
This old pain, it really ain't so painful these days

as, it seems, the end of the world was, after all, just a phase –
same way sometimes what seems a big shit turns out to be just a fart,
but then I guess that's just another of life's funny ways.

Lately, my mind don't spend so much time trotting out the malaise
and, lately, ain't so much hurt romancing anger in my heart.
This old pain, it really ain't so painful these days

and, so, maybe peace can be bought with torment, clarity with haze.
All that remains of the anguish is a fraction now, just a tiny part,
but then I guess that's just another of life's funny ways

and, as for that little leftover piece, I hope it always stays –
a keepsake of a feeling I perfected to a fine art;
this old pain, it really ain't so painful these days,
but then I guess that's just another of life's funny ways.

S.O.S.

In the swirl
of the rising wind
her hair
is a blonde tide
gushing
forth and back
from the calm
and shelter
the safety
of a harbour
out of sight
to here where
I'm beyond rescue

A Poet's Sudden Change of Fortunes

The family with the Alsatian
that never stops barking
has just moved
and taken with them
his incessant insomnia.

The weather is generally good,
great at times,
very untypical
of February and March;
rain restricted to a few minor showers.

Lately the wife and he find only petty things
to squabble over

and those strategies to cut down on
sundry expenditures
have been a gradual
but very noticeable success
– even the kids doing their bit –

and now that holiday
to wherever this August
looks just that little bit more
a possibility
if not a likelihood.

There's a new postman and he sings,
isn't half bad either;
knows pretty much everything
by Sinatra.

Even this evening
while driving home
after a relatively
stress- and complication-free day
at the office,
five of the six traffic lights
were green,
traffic itself non-existent.

It turns out Mark got a B+
on his Maths exam,
(an overwhelming improvement),
and it's finally off
between Jessica and that Thompson boy
he never approved of.

Things, he can't help noticing,
are looking up
in just about every way.

Already he's looking forward
to some time
writing nothing at all.

EDWARD O'DWYER (b. 1984), from Limerick, received his B.A. from University of Limerick and his PGDE from University College Cork, teaching English and History. He has just completed his M.A. by research in Media & Communications. In 2007, his work was published by Revival Press in the chapbook, *Revival Trio* – twelve poems together titled *Oboe*. He was selected by Poetry Ireland for their Introductions Series (2010), later that year editing the Revival Press anthology, *Sextet*. He has been shortlisted for the Hennessy Literary award for Emerging Poetry, the Desmond O'Grady Prize, the Millwheel Writers Prize, and the North West Words Prize and was nominated by the journal Gloom Cupboard for a Pushcart Prize and by Revival for a Forward Prize. In 2012, he was selected to represent Ireland at the Poesiefestival in Berlin, Germany, for a 'renshi' project involving the twenty-seven member states of Europe. He is a committee member of Cuisle Limerick City International Poetry Festival. This is his first full collection of poetry.